SIERRA AND DESERT RAILS

DONNER, FEATHER RIVER, OWENS VALLEY AT THE END OF THE STEAM AGE

by Fred Matthews

Cover Picture:
Famous Face: SP's cab-forward locos dominated Donner Pass until diesels displaced them in 1951-55. Here the last of class AC-11 (Baldwin, 1942), prepare to leave Reno for the last run of an AC over Donner, 1957.

Gotham Books

30 N Gould St.

Ste. 20820, Sheridan, WY 82801

https://gothambooksinc.com/

Phone: 1 (307) 464-7800

© 2022 Fred Matthews. All rights reserved.

No part of this book may be reproduced, stored in a retrieval system, or transmitted by any means without the written permission of the author.

Published by Gotham Books (September 9, 2022)

ISBN: 979-8-88775-042-2 (sc)
ISBN: 979-8-88775-043-9 (e)

Because of the dynamic nature of the Internet, any web addresses or links contained in this book may have changed since publication and may no longer be valid.

The views expressed in this work are solely those of the author and do not necessarily reflect the views of the publisher, and the publisher hereby disclaims any responsibility for them.

Introduction

California's railroad passes through the Sierra Nevada still draw enthusiastic observers from all over the world as I was reminded when the Professor of German Literature at Helsinki University turned up in Oakland, still excited by his walk from Truckee up to the Stanford Curve. It may be useful, therefore, to put together a record of the railroads of the Sierras in the last days of steam, which soon will have no living memories to recount.

Along with the Sierras, in the mental framework of 1950s enthusiasts, were the wondrous survivals in the desert just beyond. Most of these, even SP's Fernley and Lassen (Alturas) line, have vanished, except for a couple of magical locations in the Owens Valley. Here too, a record may be useful.

This volume is dedicated to my father, Frederic Hamilton Matthews, 1894-1952, who, by his tolerance of my early crazy train enthusiasm, made possible my life-long dedication to train photography.

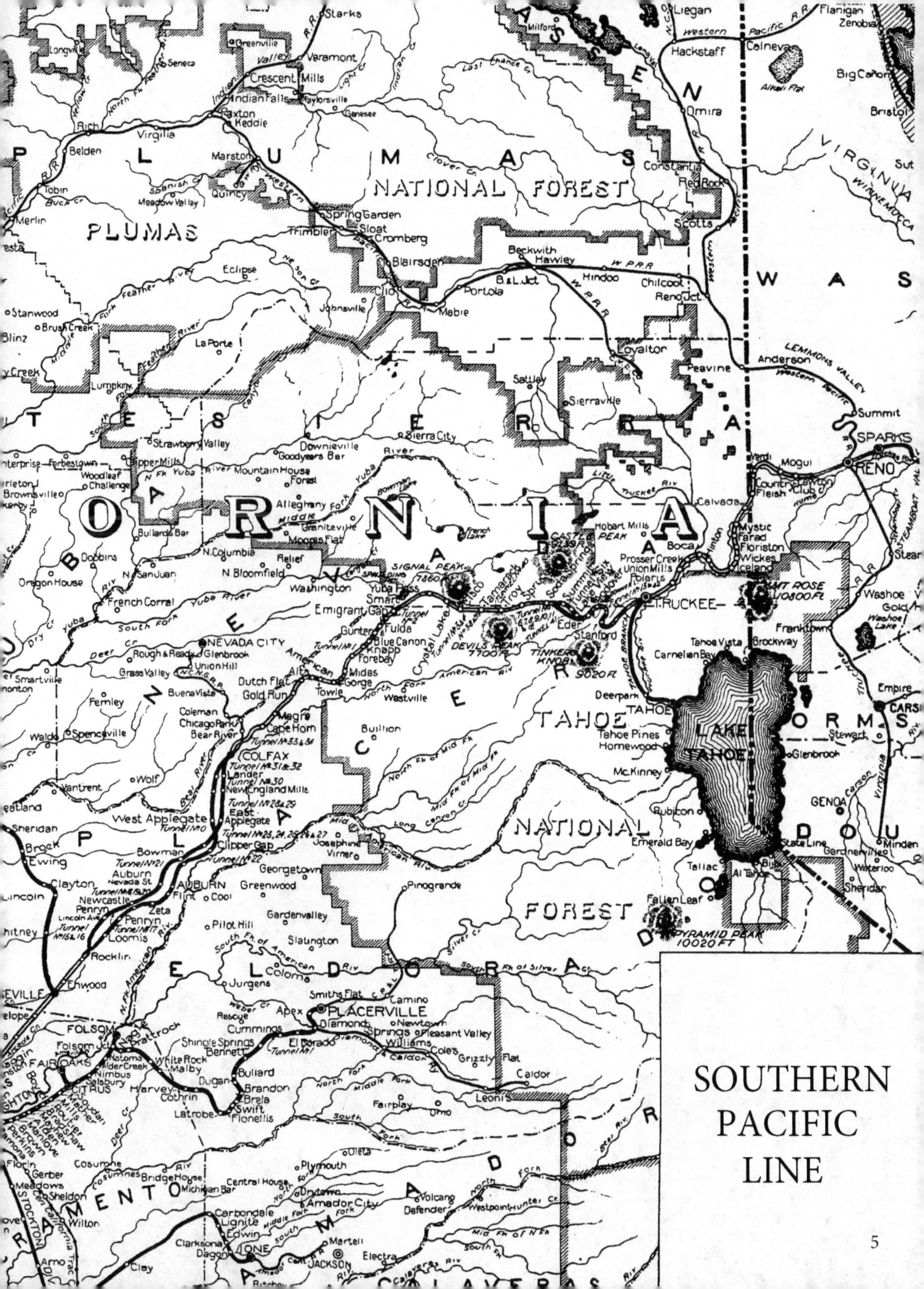

Power for the Hill, a homebuilt 4-8-2 and AC 4-8-8-2 blast off from the Roseville depot with Train 28, the S.F. Overland, on the advertised at 2.17 PM on May 13, 1950. AC-10 # 4232 of 1942 waits on the westbound to cross into Roseville yard.

Chapter 1:
ACROSS THE MOUNTAIN BARRIER: THE HILL AND THE CANYON

The single image summoned up among outlanders by the phrase "California railroads" is probably not the Valley's wedges of boxcars or the commuter parade out of San Francisco. The latter, indeed, often seemed incongruous to those whose image of California was the private auto on the freeway, just as it did to Southern Pacific's management. The mighty locomotive attacking the mountain grade in the continuing struggle to unite this wealthy state cut up by its topography had become the most familiar image of California's railroads by 1945. And, since most people and goods traveled east-west, it was the Sierra crossings, along with their southern counterpart Cajon Pass, that symbolized the state's railroads at their most splendid.

The late Forties were truly Indian Summer for the traditional operation of the two Sierra passes. Southern Pacific's steeply graded line over Donner Pass was all steam until just after 1950, with the exception of "the streamliner" City of San Francisco. Even that added a helper at Colfax eastbound until more powerful diesels came about 1948. Newcomer Western Pacific's better-graded line up the Feather River Canyon to the north had been the second in the nation to see regular diesel freight operation, but WP's tight finances delayed full dieselization through the mountains until 1951. Diesels were handling the majority of through freight to the east by 1948, but those impressive black creatures of the canyon, the M137/151 class 2-8-8-2s, ran "as required" with some frequency, especially at traffic peaks, into 1950.

And there were many traffic peaks, even before the Korean War brought a renaissance of high-value freight and of passenger specials. The explosion of America into the suburbs after 1945 meant heavy demand for Oregon and California timber; the perishable fruit and vegetable traffic still went by rail; many finished goods, including autos, came west in boxcars until regional assembly plants spread in the 50s. The main lines were busy: Southern Pacific's double track through Truckee saw strings of reefers led by the ubiquitous articulated consolidations (4-8-8-2) every hour or better on an August afternoon in 1948. And even the Western Pacific, always the challenger despite its better alignment, scheduled three time freights to the east in 1947. With frequent extras, local freights, at least two manifests for Oregon via Keddie and the Bieber connection, and the pair of daily varnish runs, Western Pacific's continuous 1% grade up the rocky canyon and then across the mountain meadows was more than busy enough to justify centralized traffic control. A rough approximation of traffic density would be seven or eight trains of all classes each way on Western Pacific west of Keddie, as compared to 25 or more thundering up Donner with two or three giant cab-forwards spaced through the train.

Double exhausts behind the westbound freight mark the Overland's hill power in action. The Daylight cars ran as parlor-observation OV-1 nd to Reno for a time after 1949.

It could almost be the third-string Gold Coast of the 1940s, running very late, but in fact it's the AC-farewell train of December 1, 1957, with brake-smoke witnessing the downgrade below Blue Canyon.

The Westbound S.F. Overland is a mile out of Truckee, on time at 12.09 PM on August 11, 1948. The 63" drivers of the big AC-10 can handle a 15-car train without helper.

An official observation car makes the westbound Overland look very traditional as it roars out of Truckee on August 11, 1948.

Pullman sleeping cars still gleamed in late spring of 1950: Train 26 is near Verdi, Nevada, where it flags at 7.05 AM. Car 260, a 10-1-2 from Oakland Pier to Reno, is joined by a sister sleeper on the eve of a Virginia and Truckee excursion.

The very last: AC-12 #4294 of 1944, only five years old, rumbles west from Reno with the Overland, due out at 11.11. AM

Solid traditional: AC-11, #4268 of 1942 brings an excursion special of Harriman coaches and tourist Pullman into Reno, running as second section of the Mail.

Lots of rail noise for the Hotel Rex in Truckee in August of 1948, with AC-11 #4274 of 1942 rolling a solid refrigerator train east.

No less than five of these eastbound runs were passenger trains well into the 1950s. According to John Signor's masterpiece Donner Pass (Golden West Books, 1985), the all-time peak was six through trains, plus some foothill locals to Colfax and briefly a couple of Truckee-Sparks In the 1940s, four of the five eastbound passengers carried sleepers, since the 10-1-2 Reno car went east on Ogden local No.26, returning on the Gold Coast which came from Chicago. Nos. 21 and 22, the Mail, had rider coaches; the City of San Francisco, S. F. Overland, and Gold Coast had a variety of sleepers plus lounges, diners and coffee shops. The Overland's Pullman lounge still boasted a barber. Only the Overlands traversed Donner by day. #25 and 26 were cut back to Sparks in 1949, but the rest remained unchanged for several years until SP's new president Donald J. Russell launched his campaign against passenger trains around 1954.

The late 1940s were the Indian summer for the great perishable trade in refrigerated boxcars, which had boomed in the Harriman years after 1900, with the formation of the SP-UP subsidiary Pacific Fruit Express in 1906 and the construction of vast icing plants at Roseville, Sparks and Ogden. In 1920 PFE had 15,000 'reefer' cars, with 8 or more solid fruit expresses per day in harvest season, on expedited schedules of 18 hours Roseville to Sparks, including mandatory safety stops plus adding and dropping helpers. Truck competition on new interstate highways, plus rail management's concern about costs, killed most of this trade after 1960, though Union Pacific is working to revive it in the 21st Century.

The experience of the two traversals of the Sierra was quite different, due in part to the points at which they challenged the mountain, in part to their ages, in part to their characteristic motive power. Heading directly east from Sacramento, the Southern Pacific ascends through the extensive, partly-wooded and rather dry foothills that typify the western slope of this huge tilted granite block. The result was miles of limited visibility except for scrub forest, "lots of trees," as someone complained. Western Pacific, until the major relocation of the early 1960s caused by the Oroville Dam project, ducked around a corner from the station there into what soon became the steep rocky canyon of the Feather's North Fork, following it for 75 miles of 1% grade compensated for curves. The grade continued along tributary creeks and upland meadows, around Williams Loop were the line twirled back across itself to keep the steady moderate grade that was designed to give this modern transcontinental line a major cost advantage in tons per unit of fuel when compared to its pioneer rival. To the scenery- seeking tourist, the Feather River Route was more continuously exciting, though the WP lacked the great vistas that punctuate the winding SP double track at Cape Horn, American, Emigrant Gap and briefly east of Donner Summit.

The face of mountain power: Extra 4212 East, with two more cab-forwards back in the train, tackles the ruling grade of 2.42% at Magra, east of Cape Horn, with the U.S. 40 bridge above. May of 1950.

A prewar cab-forward, No 4176, roaring westward up the 1% grade at Hinton, ten miles east of Truckee.

The East side allowed more frequent vistas - Donner Lake is almost visible at right as AC-10 #4241 brings reefers down into Truckee.

One long canyon: a Western Pacific freight descending the long 1% grade along the North Fork of the Feather River, above Oroville, in the summer of 1952.

Pioneer No. 2 on the second bridge west of Keddie in August of 1947, showing the more open country where the WP left the Feather's North Fork.

Some 75 miles east of Oroville, one of WP's first locos, a class C43 2-8-0 (Baldwin, 1906), scurries towards Keddie with a caboose hop. No. 2 has served for 41 years, but will soon retire.

Another WP 2-8-0 switches the west end of Keddie yard. In 1947 there was, in literal terms, no Keddie Wye; the west switch was removed, and trains for the High Line reversed and took new power in Keddie.

Above the Canyon: the westbound California Zephyr seen leaving the Williams Loop in its proud early days, 1952.

From the economic standpoint Southern Pacific's disadvantage remains. Although double-tracked and realigned in many sections from 1905 to 1925, the Donner route retains the murderous grades entailed by the desire to head directly east to the Comstock Lode and perhaps by sheer lack of knowledge of alternate routes. The Central Pacific climbs some 6,650 feet in 81 miles, if one assumes that "the Hill" begins with the 1.5% grade at Rocklin, five miles east of the present Roseville division point but itself an early helper station. Much of the grade is around 1.9%, with the lion's share of the 29 miles from Colfax to Emigrant Gap near the ruling 2.4%. (In the 1920s, an extra helper ran Colfax to Emigrant Gap). Some of the high costs were balanced by the greater capacity of the double track completed in the mid-20s. This double-tracked and realigned route boasted modern color-light signals, replacing the Harriman-era staff system.

Donner Pass in steam days, and after, was a formidable challenge to operation, especially safe operation. This was one of the longest and steepest of North American grades, on a line that had more heavy trains traversing it than other western mountain lines (perhaps excepting Cajon) until years later by which time Donner had become less busy. Retainers, to hold air in the brakes at all times, were required to be set on descending trains, beginning at the front of the train, depending on train weight and grade: one retainer for each 100M's (1000 pounds), Yuba Pass to Loomis, which included the ruling 2.42% grade, one for each 120 M's down the east side to Truckee. Locomotives had exhaust-splitters to minimize damage to snowsheds. The Employee's Timetable of February 2, 1936, noted several special safety devices. There were five eastward and four westward signals interlocked with slide fences. "Freight trains, and light engines not equipped with tire coolers,... on descending grade will stop ten minutes between switches" at Stanford, Summit, Flint (Auburn), and Norden to cool wheels; "trainmen will make careful inspection of all cars and enginemen inspect engine." Truckee, only 5½ miles down grade from Stanford, had a mandatory five minute stand. Most mountain engines had water sprays to cool wheels and discourage track fires. And there were strong warnings of the danger of letting trains roll backwards when brakes were released.

Poor visibility, especially on the 29 miles from Emigrant Gap over the top to Andover, led to an installation of Automatic Train Stop in 1927; this was extended west to Gold Run and east to Truckee in 1937. (Declining traffic, and the need to run foreign diesels through, led to its removal in 1968.) Additional refinements like operator, or dispatcher, controlled "wait" and "take-siding" indicators added capacity as freight traffic increased to around 80 trains on heavy days late in World War II.

The final trait distinguishing the two Sierra crossings was motive power. Donner Pass in 1948 meant mallets, malleys, ACs, articulated consolidations, cab-forwards, 4200s, whatever you called them, perhaps the most unique of all engine classes that came to symbolize a railroad. By no means the largest or most powerful of modern steam power, Robert LeMassena ranked them only fifteenth in potential power, they were nevertheless impressive, as the survivor in Sacramento can still demonstrate. With 523,000 lbs. weight on 63½ inch drivers, and total engine weight of 640,000 lbs., they were rated at 124,000 lbs. tractive effort. The sight of three of these distinctive beasts thundering up under U..S. 40, spaced throughout the train, was the image of California mountain railroading. Most distinctive in memory was the syncopated, whistling, "phuew-phuew" which their air pumps produced. To approach an engine terminal and hear that piercing sound multiplied by six or seven gave a sense of a camera-clad Siegfried approaching a den of many fascinating dragons.

Engine check on the east side: 65-6 4-8-4 No 4460 on downgrade at Eder, where the 1869 and 1925 lines separated, undergoing inspection, October 1958

Hard to believe: the business end of an AC at Reno, just before the last departure, December 1st, 1957. As David Morgan of Trains said, Somewhere, in another universe, there will always be an AC pounding up Donner.

Super-power is essence: the business end of one of Western Pacific's 251 class 2-8-8-2s, built by Balding in 1931 to take over the Canyon runs so older 2-6-6-2s could operate the new Northern California Extension to Bieber.

Brake smoke at Truckee, after dropping 1066 feet in 142 miles. The final AC trip, November 30, 1957.

At lonely Bieber the N.C.E. met the Great Northern's line down from the Columbia River at Wishram. An older GN 2-8-8-0 makes the connecting northbound train in August 1948. Early morning at Bieber could be wrapped in steam and smoke from a half dozen articulated and 2-10-0s; most of the day was silent.

Williams Loop One: early morning on August 31, 1947: WP's westbound Feather River Express, an all-stops local, glides around Williams Loop with a handful of passengers.

Williams Loop Two: WP 259 gaining traction around Williams Loop, August 31, 1947, by Fred Matthews Sr., with Junior on the upper level looking for a safe spot as the giant approaches. Making all the smoke because it is sanding the flues in preparation for the 7280 long tunnel at Spring Garden where Dad and I had camped the night before.

Williams Loop Three: about 15 minutes later, one of WP's newest "creature of the canyon," No. 259 of 1938, is struggling to get its eastbound time freight out of Massack siding just around the bend.

Western Pacific's opposite numbers, the 251 class locomotives built in 1931 and 1938, were as obscure as the ACs were famous. They were truly creatures of the canyon, shuttling back and forth between Oroville and Portola, with frequent runs to help out the older compound 2-6-6-2s on the new northwest connection to Bieber, completed by the James regime in 1931 to give WP an entry into north-south traffic. Never seen elsewhere, the 251s represented an extreme case of the specialization of late steam power, which made the diesel's universality all the more welcome. If anything could be, the 251s were even more impressive than the ACs. They were longer, heavier, more powerful- 549,000 pounds on 63 inch drivers, 137,000 lbs. tractive effort, or 150,900 with booster, total weight with tender a million pounds. LeMassena ranked them as the sixth most powerful engines in the abstract, and several of the higher scorers did not realize their potential. The 251s did, competing with four-unit FT diesels in power above the starting range. They lost, however, as Virgil Staff tells, us, on fuel efficiency and on starting power, thus creating scenes like that of 259 at Williams Loop.

The epic struggle of WP 259 to restart from Massack points up another trait of that long-gone epoch. Today, a dispatcher would sidetrack the passenger train for upgrade tonnage; but in 1947 traditional practice ruled, and even empty local trains held the main track. In retrospect, it's amazing that Western Pacific had only ten of these behemoths, since they are so powerfully fixed in my mind as the great western mountain power. More the pity that one did not survive into the neo-Harriman era on Western, and then Southern, Pacific, as the old rivals finally realize the Gould family's vision of a transcontinental system.

In 1948, another 251 class 2-8-8-2 brings a short westbound freight out of Spring Garden Tunnel, just above Williams Loop.

Very early on August 31, 1947, a 2-8-8-2 comes around the curve west of Spring Garden, past our camp site.

Late light, passing scene: Extra 4460 east at Boca on the final steam run, October 18, 1958.

Truly twilight; Extra 4460 departing Reno for Sparks, with worshippers all around.

Afterlife: diesel days at Truckee depot, 1986, still much track, but also much emptier as fewer trains ran through now nonstop.

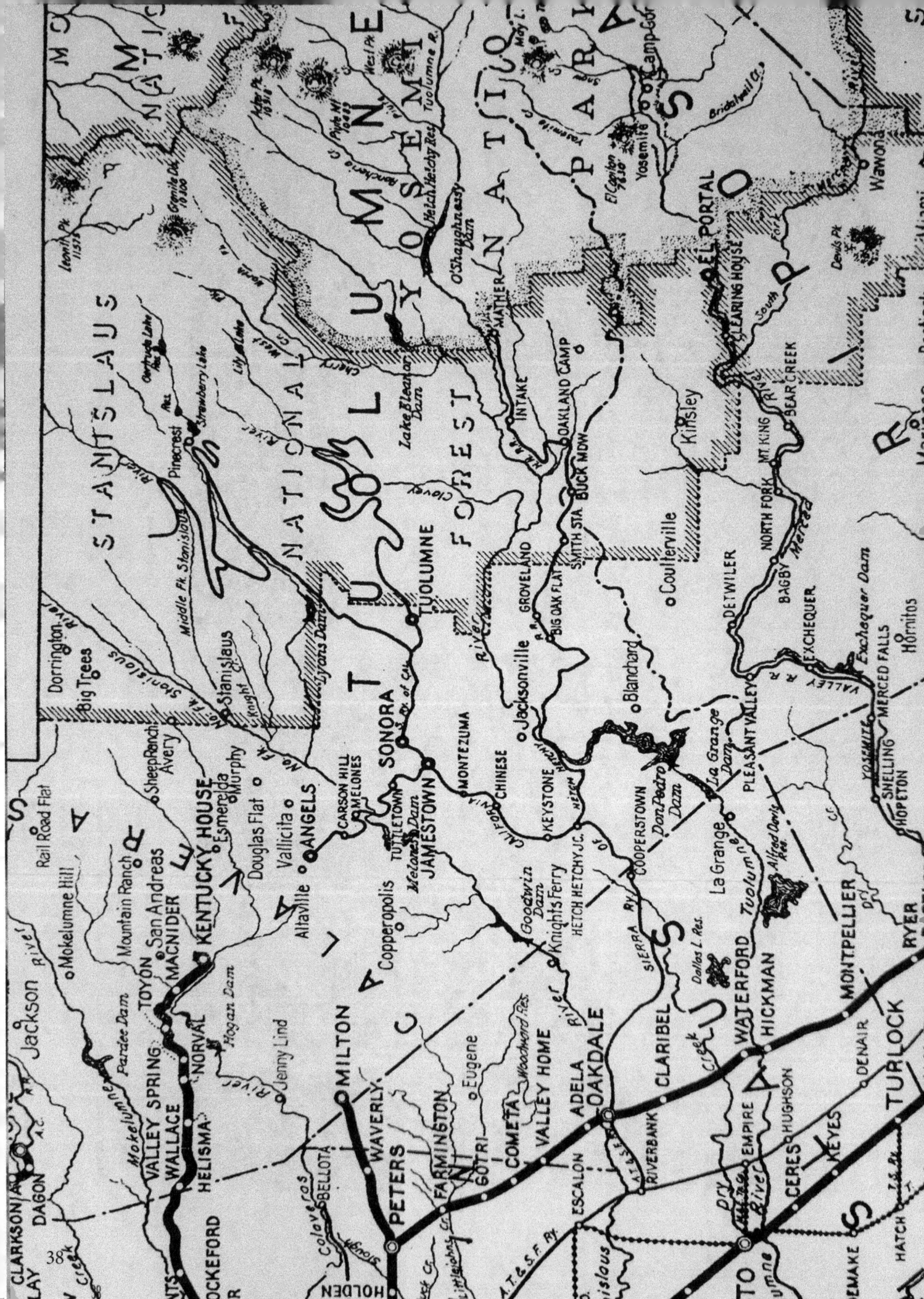

Chapter 2:
THE OAKDALE CONNECTION

The Sierra Nevada in the early 20th Century had sheltered a number of common-carrier shortlines, plus quite a few private lumber railroads, most of them short-lived since there was no traffic once the land was logged over. But there was one major exception, which lasted through and beyond the 1950s, to become a magnet for railfans. This most celebrated of California's shortline networks was what might be called the Oakdale Connection, the fan of connecting common carrier and industrial lines that radiated out from the Sierra Railroad, which in turn connects with Southern Pacific and Santa Fe branches at the quiet valley town of Oakdale. The longest of the tentacles radiating from the Sierra Railroad, San Francisco's Hetch Hetchy construction line, had ceased operating and was torn up soon after the War. But two extensive logging roads still fed the Sierra's trains.

Like other Sierra shortlines, the Sierra and its connecting lumber lines were products of the boom years between 1896 and 1914, when California expanded rapidly and the new Western Pacific and improved Southern Pacific began to open larger Eastern markets for mountain minerals and especially timber. Logging, which always generated more railroads than any other activity, had been established with the pioneer generation in the 1850s, but it generated few independent railway lines (except the components of the later Northwestern Pacific) until Eastern capital and corporations began to move west in the 1890s, and local loggers also expanded their horizons to distant markets. At the same time, timber stands easily tapped by river floats or chutes to lumber schooners were depleting, so rails began to twist inland from the rocky harbors and off the end of common-carrier branches. Another probable cause of the great proliferation was the cautious attitude of Southern Pacific after 1912 when the long legal battle began over the splitting-off of the Central Pacific. If a growing town or industry wanted a railroad, it would have to do its own. thing.

The end of the great shortline boom can be clearly marked as well; capital shortage, the good roads movement and the rapid spread of autos and trucks made a new rail line a rarity by the early 1920s, except for temporary logging trackage or rails to construction sites. The end of an era is marked by the most spectacular line that never was: when W.R. Hearst began to build his museum-palace above San Simeon in 1919, he used a fleet of ex-military Mack trucks on a winding road, instead of the geared logging lokies, or even the rack railway, that would have appeared a few years earlier.

A similar evolution took place in legal status. Until around 1920 many of the lines built to tap a single natural resource did claim common carrier status, offer passenger service and publish timetables. Sometimes this status was obtained because it entailed the right of eminent domain, the power to condemn private property for rights-of-way. Also, if a mill or processing plant was located on the short line, common carrier status would obtain a share of the through tariff on loads interchanged. But in some cases, notably the Hetch Hetchy & Yosemite Valley which ended life as the legendary West Side Lumber narrow gauge, there was no through shipment. But the pioneer promoters seem to have had visions of tourist traffic to Yosemite Park gradually developing to replace the logs as the forest retreated. From the early Twenties there was a tendency to go private, as the small passenger traffic vanished and the landmark case of the Bodie & Benton warned of the snags of common carrier status. The Bodie & Benton, an isolated lumber line in the desert near Mono Lake, had closed around 1915, following the mines it had served. The regulatory commission accepted jurisdiction on the ground that the line had accepted and charged for shipments from the general public. The abandonment was approved, but the Commission had made its case for control. Those lines that remained common carriers, like California Western and McCloud River Railroads, were shipping finished products to distant points; and in California Western's case, there was the need to serve an area of bad or no roads which supported a picturesque passenger service into the tourist era.

Aside from cut lumber, oil products and movie-filming specials, the Sierra after 1945 meant railfan excursions, often double-headed. Sometimes railfans decorated tender and even car-traps. The biggest engine built for the road, ALCO No. 36, a 2-8-2 dating to the late 1920s, heads a train of old SP cars in a scene to chill the blood of safety conscious later generations.

The Sierra Railroad's little engine terminal at Jamestown, 41 miles east of Oakdale, was unusually photogenic, nestled in the prototypically "Western" landscape that earned dollars from Hollywood movie charters. Here, in 1948, 2-8-0 No. 28 built by Baldwin in 1922 for the Sierra, rests between runs.

It could be 1920: the turn-of-century combine coach from the abandoned Angels branch is serving as caboose on a hot afternoon in September 1947. Engine 24 has hauled a cut of cars over the steep four miles to Sonora, and the crew rests while returning to Jamestown for the second cut.

Still the era of local brews, as No.24 built by Baldwin in 1913 for the Nevada Copper Belt across the mountains, heads for Tuolomne, 14 miles east of Sonora.

The Oakdale Connection became famous in part because of longevity; by the middle Fifties the two surviving loggers, Pickering and West Side, were both remarkably large operations and were becoming rarities as most other woods rails ripped up. Several of the other postwar survivors folded in the early 1950s, when California demanded standard railroad safety devices on what had been primitive operations. Both Pickering and West Side had already installed safety devices. Their very size probably also contributed to their long life; the economics of rail were improved by a sizeable haul. A major element in the lines' appeal was the Sierra Railroad's fame as a pioneer contractor for Hollywood movies, with its rolling grassy hills and live oaks forming the ideal generalized "Western "setting. And there was the sheer spectacle of the trackage: the serpentine writhings of West Side were visible on the ground as well as on topo maps, and the Pickering's line through the Stanislaus Canyon would have earned stars from Baedeker. Contrary to expectation, it was not the half-forgotten lines but the last survivors that epitomized what was most exciting about California shortlines.

The motive power of both standard-gauge Pickering and the narrow-gauge West Side had complicated histories, since they were the final sorting-out of a long game of engine-trading among several dozen logging outfits in California and Oregon. As lines were logged out, or closed for a time due to business decline, engines were sold or traded to lines with more promising futures. Pickering Shay No.8, seen on the Peeled Onion, had three prior owners after construction by Lima in 1924. Sister No.11, one of the newest and most powerful Shays, had been built in 1929 for the Forest Lumber Co. of Pine Ridge, Oregon. Some of West Side's 3-foot gauge locos had had two or even three previous owners. Several from both lines have survived, in storage or on new tourist lines that spring up, and sometimes wither.

While few of the photographers who descended on Tuolumne in the late 1950s probably knew much about it, the history of these lines was as revealing as their alignments were photogenic. All demonstrate the theme of outside capital breaking the Big Four monopoly at the turn of the century, though in this case the Crocker family of Central Pacific fame were also major financiers. Thomas Bullock was a New York entrepreneur who toured the Mother Lode country in the mid-1890s and arrived in San Francisco with news of the next gold rush: not bullion but the vast stands of virgin timber back of the old mining towns. His colorful syndicate included not only the Crockers but Prince Poniatowski of Paris, who raised French capital and inspired Oriental decoration on railway buildings. Bullock was responsible not only for the Sierra Railway of California (as it was before reorganization in the 1930s) but for both of the major lumber roads. The inner section of what became the Pickering was built as the common-carrier Sugar Pine Railway, and the West Side began life as the Hetch Hetchy & Yosemite Valley narrow gauge even as the Sierra connection from Oakdale was opened. Early promotions of the Hetch Hetchy & Yosemite Valley suggested that it had long-term plans of developing tourist traffic to Yosemite, presumably after the timber was exploited. In fact, there was little passenger service except employee and stockholder excursions, although the H H & Y V apparently ran a passenger coach on logging trains three times a week out to Nashton, later Camp 8, until Bullock sold the outfit to a Michigan lumber company in 1904. Both lines had become private operations by the early 1920s, although the Sugar Pine, now owned by Pickering Lumber, had to continue service to other shippers out on the line. For the next 40 years both roads survived (through long Depression shutdowns) into the era of nostalgia and efficient cameras, until national mergers brought them under distant managements with an eye on the bottom line. The West Side failed to reopen in 1961; the Pickering was chopped back over the next decade. But Bullock's vision of the tourist future did not die wholly; a small line has struggled to survive on the West Side out of Tuolomne; and the Sierra at Jamestown became center of a state-owned railway museum. Veterans of both lumber lines are features of tourist railways, perhaps most famously the West Side's old Heisler, which went to the new tourist line at Big Trees near Santa Cruz.

Made it: No. 24 crests the grade at Ralph, a taxing nine miles from Jamestown. This was the junction with the long, busy Pickering Lumber line, whose less-manicured track is visible at right.

The hanging pouch for water bottles was a characteristic trait of Sierra loggers; here, on the most main-line of all, Pickering Lumber No.8, from Lima in 1924 via three prior owners, as it brings a train of equipment from the woods out to the mill at the end of the logging sessions, November 3, 1956, tackling the grade up along the Peeled Onion.

The most spectacular site on California's mountain logging lines was probably the "Peeled Onion," where the Pickering Lumber's main line from backwoods branches to the mill at Ralph climbed out of the middle fork of the Stanislaus River. Modern Shay No.11 of 1929 must climb a thousand feet to Schoettgen pass before dropping 2,000 feet to Ralph, 45 rail miles ahead. It's 1958, with six years of life for this stretch of track, but a dozen for the trunk from Schoettgen to Ralph.

You can read the number: a 1923 Lima Shay passes the Tuolumne yard limit, leaving for the woods with the second of two morning consists of empty log cars.

Funny Noises in the Woods Mottled sun marked scenes of West Side's morning woods runs, here a bit beyond River Bridge led by an older Lima Shay, No. 8 of 1912.

West Side Lumber's engine terminal and mill pond at Tuolomne, in the line's last couple of years' operation around 1960.

Into the morning sun leading for Camp 8 and beyond, a train of skeleton cars fills the scrub forest with its unique chattering sound.

Not main line standard: a train of logs from the woods passes new ties in the summer of 1960 local management was still maintaining the line, but new owners decreed rail obsolete by the next Spring.

West Side No. 9 descending to River Bridge with a log train.

Blending into the woods, just beyond River Bridge.

Lots of tools on hand: No. 8 on the cliffside between River Bridge and Tuolumne.

Telephone dispatching kept the busy West Side moving. No. 8 returning to the mill, nears the Tuolumne Yard limits.

Crawling across River Bridge with a train of logs for the mill.

Chapter 3:
SURVIVORS IN THE DESERT

Beyond the passes that guided main-line rails across the Sierra came the area where nostalgia and visual grandeur were so palpable that they first became marketable commodities. The decade after 1945 saw the discovery of the mining railroads of Nevada and California's desert periphery as tourist attractions, and more broadly the great boom in Western history as a popular hobby and a saleable commodity.

It was appropriate that the desert's historic artifacts should become cult objects, since the first economic boom there in the 1860s, and the succeeding strikes that inspired rails to uncoil through unlikely terrain, had been triggered by the bonanza mentality- the lust for the pot of gold at the end of the rainbow. In this case, it was more often the bag of silver, since silver, and soon more prosaic industrial minerals that accompanied it, led the Virginia & Truckee, the Eureka Nevada and Nevada Central, the Carson & Colorado, later the Tonopah lines, to stretch out towards the heat-blurred horizon.

Agriculture, especially stock-raising, played a part later, notably with the Nevada-California-Oregon narrow gauge, which in the 1920 became SP's Alturas Line to Oregon, home of infrequent long freights dragged by massive articulateds. And the connection with Northern California was close and crucial: it was San Francisco banks and capitalists that financed the bonanza mines, and Nevada silver built many of those gingerbread mansions on Nob Hill and down the Peninsula. The old Ralston mansion in Belmont and the Flood palace on California Street survive to embody the link.

By 1945 the mining railroads were almost moribund. The Tonopah & Goldfield had survived the war on military traffic, but folded immediately after. The Nevada Copper Belt followed within two years. The remnant of the Carson & Colorado down in the Owens Valley continued to haul its talc far from the public eye. The most prominent road, running out of Reno on U.S. Highway 40 and crossing U. S. 50 at Carson City, was the Virginia & Truckee. The V & T had come close to closure just before the war, when its owner-protector died and the Mills estate moved to cut its losses. The old main line to Virginia City closed in 1938, and most of the ancient equipment was sold to Hollywood studios. Restrictions on road traffic during the war generated additional freight traffic. And just at war's end Lucius Beebe arrived in Nevada with his private railroad car and his talent for word-painting. Beebe's books and articles, and the photographs of his collaborator Charles Clegg, helped to make the Comstock in particular and the Nevada desert in general a popular travel destination, and to make a wider public aware of railroads as historic artifacts.

Even secondary main lines died in the dessert: SP'S ALTURAS cutoff, opened in the late 1920s using the right-or-way of the Nevada-California-Oregon narrow gauge, survived several temporary closures until the Union Pacific finally decided that its own Columbia River line could handle the Oregon commodities for which SP had built the Alturas line. Here, in August 1948, one of SP's first simple-articulated 4-8-8-2s heads freight for the east (but railroad-westbound) near Madeline, California, south of Alturas.

Reno still boasted a "Union Station" for a few more days in May of 1950, as one of SP's newest cab-forwards, AC-12 #4290 of 1944, blares through the numerous grade crossings, wide open for the 1% grade ahead.

Virginia Truckee No.26, a classic Baldwin ten-wheeler of 1907, brings the morning mixed out of Reno's Union Station over the Truckee River. In May of 1949 there is still some freight.

Newly-acquired No.5, heavier engine built in 1925 for the recently. abandoned Nevada Copper Belt, pauses, at Carson City en route Minden in August 1948. The purchase of this engine was mysterious, since the V & T had adequate power and No.5 hastened the deterioration of the line's light rail.

The Beebe Moment: V & T No. 26, soon to immolate herself in the Reno engine house, brings the afternoon mixed from Minden into Carson past Lucius Beebe's private car, *Gold Coast*.

Certainly the most photogenic of Western mixed trains, and much publicized by its new neighbor Lucius Beebe returning from Minden, near Washoe.

Only memories to be disturbed by the northbound mixed at Washoe, 17 miles south of Reno, in August 1948

V & T's own No. 27, with its fake wood-burner stock of the last year, leaves Washoe canyon, some 16 miles from Reno, a few days before the end in 1950.

One might single out the picture of Virginia & Truckee No.26 passing Beebe's private car as catching the moment when tourism replaced mining or ranching as the area's principal industry. No.26 was the engine that burned itself and the Reno engine house a few months before abandonment in 1950; and Beebe's presence as publisher of a weekly paper in Virginia City generated a stream of publicity for railroad and region that sustained itself after his move to the Bay Area and a Chronicle column. The otherwise unsentimental postwar management of the Virginia & Truckee recognized the new market in 1949 by fitting an ungainly balloon stack to engine No.27, built in 1913. Old had to look as old as possible, and there was a public stereotype of antiquity. Even the Southern Pacific narrow gauge miles south in the desert made the same gesture in the middle Fifties.

To this chauvinistic Californian, it was the Owens Valley line above all that summed up the grandeur of the mining roads and their environment. When one thought of "the narrow gauge" it was usually not the shrinking Colorado empire, but the antiquated little train chuffing along seventy-odd miles of sand dune and sagebrush surrounded by towering mountain escarpments. This remote remnant of the Carson & Colorado's 293 miles from a Virginia & Truckee connection at Mound House down to Keeler on Owens lake was clinging to its last few carloads of life seven decades after construction "from nowhere to nowhere." Whether powered by a steam veteran of 40 years in the desert (half of them on the old Nevada-California-Oregon to the north), or by the tiny diesel built in 1954 which was dwarfed even by a narrow gauge boxcar, the little train was the embodiment of anachronism as it bobbed along the undulant rail, tall brake wheels waving atop the cars, a trail of smoke curling from the ancient crummy's stovepipe on the hottest day in the blazing desert.

The three-foot-gauge Carson & Colorado opened in 1883, running 293 miles from the V & T at Mound House, down through the Nevada desert and over steeply-graded Mount Montrgomery Pass (which was slightly higher than Donner's 7000 feet) and down into California's Owens Valley. It was financed by a group of Comstock silver millionaires led by Darius O. Mills; but when Mills inspected the line soon after opening, he concluded that it had been built either 300 miles too long or 300 years too soon. There were traffic booms, notably a substantial flow of silver ore from Candelaria northeast of the Pass in Nevada, until the government demonetized silver in 1893. The mines along the east side of the Owens Valley had brief rebirths, but never came near to equaling the Comstock.

Water in the desert: Kearsarge Tank, ten miles north of the standard-gauge junction at Owenyo, with the ballastless 3-foot rail of the Carson & Colorado, and the Sierras' east face beyond.

After the standard-gauge line from Mojave opened in 1911 to build the Los Angeles Aqueduct, Owenyo became the narrow gauge's California operating center, and after early 1938 its only one. Looking north toward Laws, with standard gauge at left.

No. 18, one of three 4-6-0s inherited from the Nevada-California-Oregon in the late Twenties, is busy next to the standard gauge engine from Mojave. Although looking newer and much heavier, Mikado 3203 dated from the same year as No. 18, 1911.

Aberdeen, 23 miles north of Owenyo, still has talc cars to shunt in February 1951, with the Sierra behind.

Talc is being loaded at Zurich, 37 miles north of Owenyo and 17 south of Laws. Snow on the bone-dry White Mountains indicates it's winter.

At Laws, February 1952: shunting to make up the southbound train. Car 401 was later rebuilt with flat roof. It had come from the South Pacific Coast line in the Bay Area after that was standard-gauged in 1906.

End of the line: turning No.18 in traditional style at Laws.

The tri-weekly freight ready to leave Laws in February 1952. On three other days a train ran Owenyo, Aberdeen (or Zurich), Keeler, Owenyo.

The narrow-gauge contracted in periodic segments. With the Tonopah boom after 1904, the break of gauge became a major nuisance, so the SP, which had bought the C&C in 1900, built a cutoff from Hazen on their main line, and regauged the three-foot to the new Tonopah Junction. A few miles of 3-rail track allowed the sparse service over Mt Montgomery, usually less than daily, to reach the division point at Mina. This arrangement lasted until 1938, with some seasonal stock extras behind triple-headers. The pass went in '38, then another section from Benton to Laws as wartime scrap.

A little mineral traffic lingered into the 1940s, and a watered stockyard survived at Laws in the 1955 employees' timetable, but the major flow was talc for the Sierra Talc works at Keeler. Perhaps the line's most notable flow had been marble from the Inyo Marble Works 5 miles above Keeler, to build the grand (D.O.) Mills Building, finished 1890, that still stands in San Francisco's financial district.

The Owens Valley framed the train perfectly. Legally part of California, topographically kin to Nevada, a microcosm of much of Western history, it is hemmed in by the sheer escarpment of the Sierra Nevada on the west and the lower Inyos and Whites barren and blistering on the east. Mount Whitney, almost 15,000 feet high, loomed over the line south of Owenyo; there were several nearby Sierra peaks over 14,000. The bone-dry Inyos to the east rose to over 11,000 feet. The valley floor descended gently from about 4100' at Laws to near 3600' around Owens lake, which still floated steamboats in the 1880s.

Crossing the Owens River on one of two trestles added when the line was relocated around L.A. Water and Power's Tinemaha Reservoir in the 1920s.

Just below Tinemaha the relocated line has swung west toward the Sierras. SP "caboose" 12, like sister 401, had come from the South Pacific Coast.

Southbound on the "new" line next to Tinemaha Reservoir.

Dramatic winter light at Tinemaha in 1951.

The severe desert began near Aberdeen, though remnants of cultivation are visible at the left in this transition zone.

Still the 1890s at Kearsarge depot, where passengers for the town of Independence, a couple of miles west, would have detrained. The Carson & Colorado had avoided the Owens valley settlements to minimize land costs and go close to likely or actual mines.

A drink in the desert at Kearsarge Tank, 1951

Rush Hour at Owenyo: by July 1959 the annual interval of steam operation brought photographers from far afield

Leaving Owenyo for Keeler

The Owens Valley had not always been so bleak and empty as in the 1950s. Here was enacted one of the archetypical dramas of Western history. High in the mountains on both sides of the valley are the remnants of dozens of mines, pioneer operations that paved the way for the major lead-zinc-silver operations at the Cerro Gordo near Keeler and its companions, and still later for the prosaic pits producing talc which kept the railway running until 1960. But soon after the miners came ranchers and farmers; by 1900 the Owens Valley was a lush, thriving agricultural area. Shortly after 1900 the great water battle began: Los Angeles bought up water rights, urged the federal government to abandon irrigation projects, and built an aqueduct to drain the valley's water away to the metropolis. After a long legal struggle and sporadic dynamiting of the aqueduct, the residents capitulated and most left the valley to dry out. As the little train rattled along the northern half of its dusty path across the face of the moon, it passed the remnants of fertile farms and flowing streams. A number of ranches remained, but the valley's face bore the ravages of its defeat. Even more striking changes had occurred at Owens Lake, in the permanent desert near Keeler. By the 1930s only salt flats reflected the blinding sun where steamers plied in the previous century.

While it was known to enthusiasts, and articles about it did appear in travel journals, in general the Owens Valley line lived out its final decade in splendid solitude. The little towns of the valley served the remaining ranchers, outfitted vacationers to the Sierra wilderness to the West, and broke the monotony for truckers and tourists racing along U.S. 395 between Reno and L.A. (Briefly, during the War, they had as neighbors the Japanese relocation camp at Manzanar, but that was gone and not discussed in the Fifties.) All but a few of those travelers along 395 dashed on through, never suspecting that over at the base of the Inyos and Whites was the last direct link with the Homeric days of Western mining and railroading. When Southern Pacific finally proposed replacement by oversize trucks at the end of the 50s, there was only one proposal for a tourist operation, and financing did not appear. It was a long way from anywhere. On April 21, 1960, the Owenyo agent sent out cards: "The last run of the N.G. will be on April 29, 1960 when all cars will be brought in from Keeler, Calif. And Laws, Calif. and the line abandoned."

The minimalist right-of-way has largely vanished, some if it used for dirt roads. Two survivors remain: an engine and cars on a short piece of track at Laws, and the few lengths of rail left under the Death Valley Highway south of Owenyo, a fitting memorial seen against its Sierra backdrop.

Just a year of life ahead on May 17, 1959 as "little giant," the tiny diesel purchased in 1954 to replace aging steam power, approaches the Old Death Valley Highway crossing south of Owenyo, en route to Keeler.

Land of infinite solitude: unchanged for decades except for its diesel, the narrow-gauge would leave few traces behind. Heading towards Mount Whitney station and Keeler on May 17, 1959.

The San Joaquin Division employee's timetable warned, "Look out for blowing sand between MP 573 and MP 575." Here, in February 1951, the warning is justified as graceful old No. 18 approaches Mt. Whitney siding en route Keeler.

On its final tour of duty in July 1959, while Little Giant was off being repaired, No.9 steams sedately into Keeler in frying heat. Unnecessary tracks are already gone, but a surprising number of sheds and other rail stigmata remained visible here in the late 1990s.

The business of the line, still substantial: looking south from Keeler station to the Sierra Talc works at Keeler, July 17, 1959.

Owens lake remnants: No.9 at an unloader behind the Sierra Talc works south of Keeler, with the stub of the old branch to the Owens lake steamer dock at right. July 17, 1959.

Slow motion: No.9 rolling over the unballasted rail on the return from Keeler to Owenyo.

Returning to Owenyo, with the bone-dry Inyo Mountains hiding defunct mines behind

Diesel No.1 heading for Keeler near Mt. Whitney station and peak, May 1959.

TRAIN ORDER No. 1028   JULY 17 195

To C & E   ENG 9

NO 702

At   OWENYO   X   Opr.   M.
        STATION

ENG 9 WORKS EXTRA 701 AM UNTIL 1050 PM

BETWEEN KEELER AND LAWS

NOT PROTECTING AGAINST EXTRA TRAINS

Repeated and Complete Time   M

Impressive survival: Death Valley Highway crossing, about 1997.

www.ingramcontent.com/pod-product-compliance
Lightning Source LLC
LaVergne TN
LVHW062047070526
838201LV00080B/2112